Crestwood House

SPORTS HEADLINERS

TROY AIKMAN

CARL R. GREEN

CRESTWOOD HOUSE
NEW YORK
MAXWELL MACMILLAN CANADA
TORONTO
MAXWELL MACMILLAN INTERNATIONAL
NEW YORK   OXFORD   SINGAPORE   SYDNEY

Photo Credits:
All photos courtesy of AP—WIDE WORLD PHOTOS.

Cover design, text design, and production: William E. Frost Associates Ltd.

Library of Congress Cataloging-in-Publication Data

Green, Carl R.
  Troy Aikman / by Carl R. Green.—1st ed.
    p. cm.—(Sports headliners)
    Includes bibliographical references (p.) and index.
    Summary: A biography of Dallas Cowboy hero
Troy Aikman.
    ISBN 0-89686-833-8
    1. Aikman, Troy, 1966– —Juvenile literature. 2.
Football players—United States—Biography—
Juvenile literature. 3. Dallas Cowboys (Football
team)—Juvenile literature. [1. Aikman, Troy, 1966-
2. Football players.] I. Title. II. Series.
GV939.A46G74   1994
796.332′092—dc20
[B]   93-17480

CRESTWOOD HOUSE
MACMILLAN PUBLISHING COMPANY
866 Third Avenue
New York, NY 10022

MAXWELL MACMILLAN CANADA, INC.
1200 Eglinton Avenue East
Suite 200
Don Mills, Ontario M3C 3N1

Macmillan Publishing Company is part of the Maxwell Communication Group of Companies.

Printed in the United States of America
First edition

10 9 8 7 6 5 4 3 2 1

Contents

Football experts and fans feel that Troy Aikman's playing is second to none.

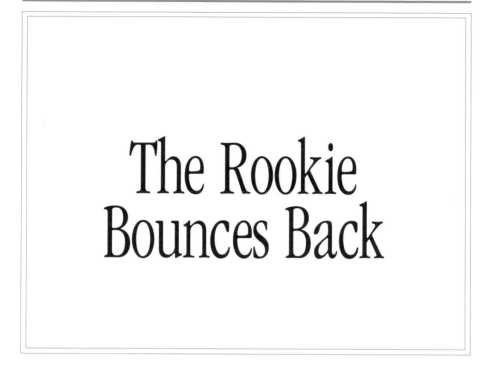

Chapter 1

The Rookie Bounces Back

The first four games of 1989 had been a nightmare. Instead of setting the National Football League on fire, the young quarter-back had gone down in flames. Opposing teams had picked off six of his passes, and he had been the victim of a **sack** six times. He threw only one touchdown (TD) pass before breaking his finger.

Five games slipped by while Troy Aikman's finger healed. Now, nine games into their season, the Dallas Cowboys had won only once. Coach Jimmy Johnson picked Troy to start the November 12 game against the Phoenix Cardinals. Troy knew he had played like a nervous **rookie** during the first four games. After the layoff he felt more relaxed.

For the first time as a pro, Troy took command. Two field goals and a 5-yard TD pass gave the Cowboys a 13–7 lead at halftime. But Tom Tupa, the Cardinals' backup quarterback, led two second-half scoring drives. With less than two minutes to play, Dallas trailed, 13–17.

The Cowboys took over on their own 25-yard line. Troy took the snap, dropped back, and saw James Dixon break into the clear. As Troy threw the ball, a Phoenix linebacker smashed him to the ground. Troy went down hard, but his pass was on target. The speedy Dixon raced into the end zone to complete a 75-yard scoring play.

Troy lay on the grass, blood oozing from his right ear. When he wobbled to his feet, he looked dazed. "I was knocked out. I didn't know what happened until Coach Johnson told me just before I got off the field," Troy said later. A doctor told him that he had a mild concussion.

With only 1 minute 43 seconds left, the Cowboys thought they had the game wrapped up, 20–17. Tupa had other ideas. He stormed back with a 72-yard bomb of his own. The TD pass gave Phoenix a 24–20 comeback win. Troy had passed for 379 yards, but it wasn't enough. The hard-luck Cowboys were on their way to a 1–15 season.

Football experts later called the Phoenix game a turning point despite the loss. The rookie quarterback had proved he was tough as well as talented. Forget the 1989 season, they said. Troy Aikman was born to lead Dallas to the Super Bowl.

Chapter 2

Growing Up in Two Worlds

Troy Kenneth Aikman did not look like a future superstar when he was born November 21, 1966. Charlyn and Ken Aikman's only son had a slight birth defect. The problem was later diagnosed as "one-third **club foot**." The Aikmans discussed the problem with the doctors at the West Covina, California, hospital. Then they took the baby home to meet his sisters, Tammy and Terri.

Eight months later a doctor put casts on both of Troy's legs. The casts, which kept his feet straight, stayed on until he started walking five months later. At that point the doctor removed the

7

casts and fitted the toddler for **orthopedic shoes.** Troy wore those heavy, awkward shoes 24 hours a day until he was three. By then he could walk and run like the other three-year-olds.

Ken worked in the oil fields as a pipe fitter. He passed on his ideas about life to his blond-haired, blue-eyed son. A man, Troy learned, doesn't whimper, complain, or cry. He gives an honest day's work for a day's pay. Friends, family, and church come first. The Aikmans also made sure that their children did their schoolwork and helped with the chores.

After several moves, the family settled in the Los Angeles suburb of Cerritos. Troy was a happy-go-lucky, sports-loving kid. He hadn't thought about playing tackle football—but then he fell in love. At that time Tammy and Terri were cheerleaders for a junior **All-American** football team. While he was watching the Hornets play one day, a peppy blond cheerleader caught Troy's eye. "Carla was beautiful," he remembers.

He decided to try to win Carla's love by playing football! Luckily, the Hornets fielded a team for his age group. During tryouts the coach picked Troy to play quarterback. When the 5-foot 7-inch 9-year-old weighed in at 110 pounds, the coaches pulled out the rule book. Troy had to lose 10 pounds to make the weight limit. He lost 11 pounds in two weeks, but felt "sick as a dog."

Troy mastered the running, throwing, and ball-handling skills required of a quarterback. He impressed the coaches, but he did not impress Carla. Seventh-grade girls, he discovered, do not notice fourth-grade boys.

The one-sided romance ended in 1979. Ken moved his family to a 172-acre ranch outside of Henryetta, Oklahoma. Twelve-year-old Troy hated the move at first. Henryetta, a town of 6,000, did not have a mall or a McDonald's in those years. But Troy soon discovered that small-town life has its own pleasures. He went fishing, played peewee football, and listened to country music. "Within a couple of months it felt like I had lived there my whole life," he says.

Those who know Troy believe that his personality is even more remarkable than his football skills.

The people of Henryetta loved their youth sports teams. Troy never learned to ride a horse, but he played each sport in season. Success on the football field led him to think that sports might be his ticket to fame. "As a kid I used to practice my signature," he says. "I'd say to myself, 'One day I'll be somebody. They'll want my autograph. They'll want me to do Gatorade commercials.'"

The endorsements would have to wait, however. First he had to make the team at Henryetta High School.

Strength, speed, and accuracy are some of the qualities
that make Troy an awesome quarterback.

The Fighting Hens

Henryetta High School ran an active athletic program. Tall, strong, and agile, Troy went out for each sport in season. He played quarterback for the football team, center for the basketball squad, and shortstop on the baseball team. All three sports were popular, but football was king. The townsfolk prayed each year that their Fighting Hens would make the state **play-offs**.

The team's nickname may have been part of the problem. Opponents, Troy and his teammates said, did not take the Fighting Hens seriously. The players went to the school board and asked for a name change. The board listened—and turned them down. As Troy tells the story, "All the old codgers in town said, 'Hell, no, if we had to put up with it, so do [you].'" In 1989, long after Troy graduated, the "old codgers" did give in. Henryetta's teams are now known as the Knights.

Troy earned the first of four letters in baseball during his freshman year. He is remembered for a home run that cleared the fence and hit the nearby Wal-Mart. In 1982, as a sophomore, he moved in as the varsity quarterback. In a game against the Checotah Wildcats, he threw a game-winning 60-yard touchdown pass. When Okmulgee State Technical School held a typing contest, Troy entered that, too. Principal Rick Ennis remembers that Troy was the only male out of 38 entrants. Always a competitor, Troy won the contest.

With Troy at quarterback, Henryetta looked forward to a winning season in 1983. That was the year the Fighting Hens nearly laid an egg. After eight games the team was still looking for its first win. Then, spurred by Troy's running and passing, the Hens won their next two games. The sudden spurt earned the team a place in the state play-offs. The local fans were overjoyed, even though the Hens lost in the first round.

In Troy's senior year the Hens improved to 6–4. Troy earned All-Conference and All-State honors. The popular newspaper *USA Today* named him to its honorable mention All-American high school team. Those honors were well deserved. During his high school career Troy passed for 3,208 yards and 30 touchdowns. He also rushed for 1,568 yards and 15 touchdowns. When his heroics did not produce a state title, the school board fired the coach. By then the people of Henryetta were expecting miracles.

Troy's football talents, combined with his good grades, caught the attention of college coaches. At first, Troy leaned toward Oklahoma State. The state Cowboys, he knew, favored a passing game. But then he spent a few days at the University of Oklahoma, in Norman. Coach Barry Switzer told Troy that the Sooners were giving up their run-happy **wishbone offense**. He described a new scheme that would feature drop-back passes.

Troy at work for the Oklahoma Sooners

"In the state of Oklahoma, OU football is everything," Troy says. "Everybody wants to go to OU." Caught up in the fever, Troy accepted Switzer's offer of a **football scholarship**. "Deep down," he says, "I wanted to believe they were going to throw the football."

Troy graduated from high school with his class of 100 that spring of 1984. When fall came, he packed his blue jeans and cowboy boots and left for Norman. He was excited about playing football, but it wasn't his only ambition in life. Troy was also planning to go to medical school.

As a college freshman, Troy found that playing football and earning high grades was much more demanding than in high school.

Chapter 4

A Broken Bone and a Broken Promise

Troy's plans changed almost as soon as he arrived at OU in 1984. He found that he could not pursue a pre-med major while playing football. "The practices, the meetings were too time-consuming," he remembers. "I had to go into something more manageable." After trying business management, he settled on sociology.

The next surprise was more troubling. Coach Switzer changed his mind about switching to a wide-open offense. Instead, he added a few more pass plays to the wishbone. In that formation the quarterback's main job was to pitch the ball to OU's speedy halfbacks. "The only real difference," Troy says, "was that we threw the ball 12 times a game instead of 7."

The broken promise upset Troy, but he was not a quitter. "If I had been playing, I would have stayed," he says. It took a series of mishaps to drive him away.

At major football schools, freshmen often sit out their first year. Troy welcomed this **"redshirt" year** as a time to adjust to college life. But then OU's quarterback went down with an injury. After sitting out the first six games, Troy was called on to start against Kansas. The results did not make for good reading back in Henryetta. Troy completed only two passes—and gave up three **interceptions**. Switzer defended his quarterback after the 28–11 loss. "Our whole team laid down that day and didn't give Troy any help," he said.

Troy took a lot of heat from OU fans, but he did not give up. He came back in 1985 and earned the starting job. In his first three games he completed 21 of 40 passes for 317 yards. But Jamelle Holieway, a born wishbone quarterback, was coming on fast. Troy knew that Switzer wanted to give the freshman more playing time. He worried that he might be benched if he had a bad game.

The end came just when the future looked bright. Troy opened the Miami game by completing six of seven passes. Then a broken ankle ended the hot streak in the second quarter. Holieway took over at quarterback and never looked back. The Sooners rode the wishbone to an Orange Bowl win and a national championship. Troy leaned on his crutches and watched from the sidelines.

Spring drills convinced Troy that Holieway had a lock on the starting job. If he stayed, he would most likely ride the bench for two years. After that, would a big-time team risk a **pro draft** pick on him? It was a long shot at best. Troy made up his mind to leave Oklahoma.

To Troy's surprise, Switzer welcomed his request. The coach picked up the phone and called some friends. His calls opened doors at Stanford University, Arizona State, and the University of California at Los Angeles. When UCLA coach

Terry Donahue offered a scholarship, Troy said yes. He liked the idea of playing in UCLA's pro-type offense.

OU played UCLA in the 1986 season opener. After the game, as the coaches had agreed, Troy enrolled at UCLA. When he joined the workouts, his new coach saw him in action for the first time.

"When I saw him move around, I finally started to get excited," Donahue says. "That's when I began to feel we had gotten something special."

Troy brought a sharp eye and strong passing arm to the
UCLA Bruins.

Chapter 5

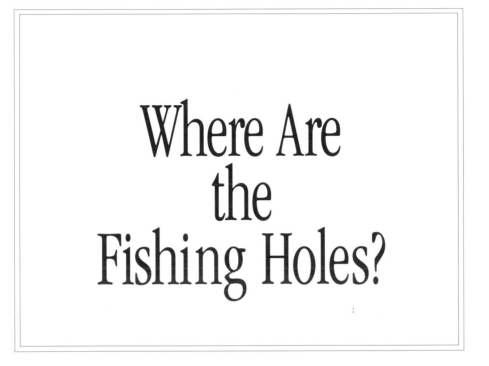

Where Are the Fishing Holes?

A college athlete who switches schools must sit out for a year. The rule meant that Troy could practice, but he could not suit up for games. Away from the field, he went to classes, drove his pickup, and studied the UCLA playbook. "I haven't fished once out here," he teased his new friends. "I don't even know where you'd go."

Along with brains and good humor, Troy had size and strength. At 6 feet 4 inches and 220 pounds, he looked big enough to play tight end. In the UCLA weight room he set a leg press record of 640 pounds for quarterbacks.

Coach Donahue asked Rick Neuheisel to work with Troy. Neuheisel, a former quarterback, took on the task gladly. His prize pupil threw pinpoint passes and ran the 40 in a fast 4.69 seconds. What Troy lacked was practice in reading defenses. Neuheisel drilled him in finding the open man when his primary receiver was covered.

During spring drills Troy showed he had the right stuff. His calm, take-charge attitude inspired confidence in his linemen. Receivers loved his strong arm. They knew he could deliver the ball to them anywhere on the field. When fall 1987 came, Coach Donahue named him to start the first game.

Troy responded by hitting 8 of 10 passes in a 47–14 win over San Diego State. At that point, the Bruins were rated number 3 in the nation. Matched against number 2 Nebraska, they lost a wild game, 42–33. Despite the loss, the Bruins felt good afterward. They had almost beaten the mighty Huskers on their own field.

Led by Troy's passing and the running of Gaston Green, UCLA rolled over its next eight opponents. In those ten games Troy threw for 2,183 yards and 16 touchdowns. Only arch-rival USC stood between the Bruins and the Rose Bowl.

More than 92,000 fans packed the Los Angeles Coliseum on November 21. It was Troy's birthday, but it was not a day for celebration. The Bruins took a 13–3 lead into the third quarter but could not hold it. The Trojans turned two interceptions into touchdowns and went ahead, 17–13. Troy tried to rally his team, only to throw a drive-killing third interception.

The upset put USC in the Rose Bowl. UCLA took second best, a bid to play the University of Florida in the Aloha Bowl. Troy completed 19 of 30 passes as UCLA held on for a 20–16 victory. The win raised the Bruins to number 9 in the national rankings.

The honors came rolling in. Troy was named a second-team All-American. He was runner-up to Don McPherson of Syracuse for the Davey O'Brien National Quarterback Award. As the awards piled up, the football world waited. Would the UCLA star turn pro?

Coach Terry Donahue is carried by team members after a
Bruins victory.

Troy refused to be swept up in the hype. He said he was
staying at UCLA. Asked about the pro draft, he said, "It was just
something I felt wouldn't be right. I made a commitment for two
years. I think leaving would tarnish the game."

Coach Donahue was delighted. With Troy at quarterback,
the Bruins would have another shot at the Rose Bowl.

Troy warms up during a UCLA practice session.

Chapter 6

An All-American Year

A scholarship pays for school costs, but the money stops during vacations. Following in his dad's footsteps, Troy worked on a pipeline during the summer of 1988. The hot, heavy work taught him a lesson. "Now I know what I won't do with my life," he says.

Working pipeline was typical of Troy. Some California football players "go Hollywood," dating models and driving flashy sports cars. Troy rejected that role. He was just "one of the guys" on the pipeline crew. At UCLA he spent his free time with the team's blue-collar workers, the linemen. "I'm not a guy who needs the spotlight," he said.

Sportswriters warned that the autumn of 1988 would be a rebuilding period for the Bruins. The offensive unit had only four returning starters. The doubts turned to cheers as UCLA rode Troy's passing to seven straight wins. The biggest was a 41–28 upset win over number 2 Nebraska. The Bruins broke the game open with 28 points in the first quarter. Troy chipped in with two touchdown passes during the scoring spree.

For seven weeks the Bruins ruled the college football world. At halftime the eighth game looked like one more blowout. Then, in the third quarter, Washington State caught fire. Helped by Bruin mistakes, the Cougars scored 21 straight points to tie the score. UCLA countered with a field goal, but Washington State scored another touchdown. Trailing 30–34, Troy marched the Bruins to the Cougar 6-yard line. With no time-outs left, he had to throw the ball away to stop the clock.

With the seconds ticking off, UCLA called three straight pass plays. The home crowd groaned as each pass fell incomplete. The game ended moments later. The upset knocked UCLA out of the number 1 spot in the ratings.

The Bruins came back to win the next two games. That set the stage for the yearly grudge match against USC. The Trojans were 9–0 and ranked number 2. To heighten the drama, both teams were led by star quarterbacks. Troy and USC's Rodney Peete were candidates for college football's highest honor, the Heisman Trophy.

Five days before the game, Peete came down with the measles. Somehow he climbed out of bed in time to play on Saturday. His return inspired the Trojans. UCLA kicked 3 first-half field goals, but USC scored 3 touchdowns. Troy led drive after drive, only to come up short against the Trojan defense. He hit on 32 of 48 passes, good for 317 yards and 2 touchdowns. It wasn't enough. USC won, 31–22.

Locked out of the Rose Bowl again, UCLA accepted a bid to the 1989 Cotton Bowl. Troy ended his college career on New Year's Day against Arkansas. He hit on 19 of 27 passes as the Bruins smothered the Razorbacks, 17–3.

The win boosted the Bruins to a number 6 ranking. Troy's

NFL Commissioner Pete Rozelle (right) announces the selection of Troy Aikman as first pick by the Dallas Cowboys.

season stats added up to 2,771 passing yards and 24 touchdowns. Those superb numbers were not enough to win the Heisman. Troy finished third, behind Peete and the winner, Barry Sanders of Oklahoma State.

The UCLA star did pick up two big honors. The first gave him a handsome trophy—the Davey O'Brien National Quarterback Award. The second added some big bucks to his bank account. Picking first in the NFL draft, the Dallas Cowboys chose Troy Aikman.

Troy takes a dive for Dallas as he is tackled by Reggie White of the Philadelphia Eagles.

Chapter 7

Breaking In with the Cowboys

The 1988 Dallas Cowboys were a pale shadow of the team that had played in five Super Bowls. Jerry Jones bought the franchise and fired coaching legend Tom Landry. The $140 million he paid for the Cowboys gave him the right to choose his own coach, he said. Jones hired Miami's Jimmy Johnson and opened his checkbook.

Leigh Steinberg, Troy's **agent**, worked out a six-year, $11.2 million deal with Jones. Troy signed the contract on April 20, 1989. His yearly salary was set to top out at $1.287 million in 1994. A stroke of the pen turned the pipe fitter's son into a millionaire.

The Cowboys knew about Troy's arm strength and passing

27

skills. The team's **scouts** said that he had other talents as well. He's mentally and physically tough, the reports said. Troy isn't a **scrambler**, the scouts added, but he's hard to sack. His quick release lets him avoid most pass rushers. The reports compared him with the great Joe Namath—but without Joe's bad knees.

Training camp opened near the end of the summer. Off the field, the veterans made the rookies run errands and sing before meals. Troy took the team's initiation rituals with good grace. On the field, he competed with Steve Walsh for the starting job. Troy had the better arm, but Walsh had a fine feel for the game. Playing for Coach Johnson at Miami, Walsh had lost only one game in two years.

The two rookies shared playing time during the practice season. Then, with the regular season about to start, Johnson made his choice. He sent Troy in at quarterback against the New Orleans Saints on September 10. The Saints promptly threw every defense in the book at the rookie. Troy completed 17 of 35 passes but could not put points on the scoreboard. The Cowboys lost, 28–0.

The losing streak soon stretched to four in a row. Still shaky, Troy completed only six passes in a game against the Washington Redskins. The next week he went out with a broken finger. Walsh stepped in and managed one win, a rematch with the Redskins. Troy came back five weeks later and turned his season around against Phoenix. His 379 passing yards in that game almost doubled his yardage for the first four games. More to the point, his teammates accepted him as their leader on offense.

Even though Troy improved week by week, the Cowboys ended the year 1–15. Some key players went down with injuries, including **wide receiver** Michael Irvin. Caught up in the turmoil of the coaching change, others played poorly. The losses hurt, but Troy's play gave Cowboy fans hope for the future. In 11 games Troy completed 155 of 293 passes for 1,749 yards and 9 touchdowns. Forced to scramble out of the **pocket** more than was wise, he also gained 302 yards on the ground.

As a rookie, Troy gained the confidence and control that was needed to turn Dallas into a winning team.

At season's end, Troy's body was battered and bruised. "I don't know how those quarterbacks make it ten years," he moaned.

Coach Johnson was already looking to the future. He assured Troy that he had played far better than expected. The team would get Troy some help, Johnson added.

Troy searches for an open receiver during the last quarter of a game against San Diego.

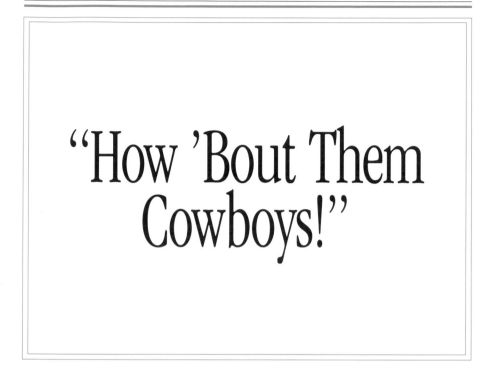

Chapter 8

"How 'Bout Them Cowboys!"

Coach Johnson chose running back Emmitt Smith as the fourteenth pick in the 1990 draft. The teams that overlooked him soon knew they had made a mistake. Smith gave the Cowboys a running threat to balance the passing game. Troy felt even better when his old rival Steve Walsh was traded to New Orleans.

The 1990 season proved that the Cowboys were on the right track. The team opened with a hard-fought win over San Diego. Troy scored the winning touchdown on a 1-yard sneak with 1 minute 58 seconds left in the game. Then, matched against the NFL's best, the Cowboys lost seven of their next nine.

The losses stopped in a game with the Los Angeles Rams. Troy started the turnaround by throwing for three quick touchdowns. He capped it with a last-minute, 89-yard drive to a winning field goal. Four days later he beat the Redskins with two fourth-quarter drives. Next came New Orleans, now led by Walsh. This time Troy engineered drives of 80 and 50 yards to beat the Saints. At one point he clicked on 11 straight passes. A week later at Phoenix the team won its fourth straight game.

The Cowboys lost their win streak and their quarterback in Philadelphia on December 23, 1990. A shoulder injury knocked Troy out for the rest of the season. Another loss the next week spoiled the team's hopes of making the play-offs. Even so, their 7–9 record stamped the young Cowboys as a team to watch.

The 1991 off-season was a busy one for Troy. First came surgery to repair his shoulder. Next came the task of adjusting to a new coach. Norv Turner, hired to run the offense, changed the team's passing style to fit Troy's strengths. Drop back seven steps, set up in the pocket, and fire the ball, he told his quarterback. "We tried to have him throw most things a lot quicker," Turner explains.

A barrage of short passes paid off with a win in the first game. Troy's receivers gathered in 24 passes, good for 274 yards. A week later the Cowboys were outgunned in a loss to the Redskins. Troy kept the passing game in gear with 27 completions against the future Super Bowl champs.

After a loss to Philadelphia, the Cowboys started a four-game win streak. The highlight was a come-from-behind win over the New York Giants. The victory earned NFL Offensive Player of the Week honors for Troy. He returned seven days later and completed a career-high 31 passes against Green Bay.

Just when the road to the play-offs looked clear, the Cowboys skidded. Three losses in the next four games dropped the team's record to 7–5. Then the injury jinx hit again. Troy injured his right knee in a rematch with the Redskins. Steve Beuerlein, his backup, finished the game. Troy did not play again until the second round of the play-offs.

With Beuerlein at the controls, the Cowboys finished 11–5.

The passing arm of Troy Aikman is one of the Cowboys' greatest offensive weapons.

That was good enough to earn a **wild card** spot in the play-offs. In the first play-off game Dallas beat Chicago, 17–13. Now the team was only two games away from the Super Bowl. The Detroit Lions ended the dream a week later, 38–6. Troy played in the second half, but neither Cowboy quarterback could muster a scoring punch.

Dallas fans were not dismayed. "How 'bout them Cowboys!" they yelled.

Number 8 scrambles to escape the grasp of Eagles' player
Mike Pitts.

Chapter 9

America's Team
Is Back

Back in 1979, the Dallas Cowboys were known as "America's Team." Football fans from coast to coast loved—or hated—the winners from Texas. But the glory of five trips to the Super Bowl faded in the 1980s.

In 1992 the nickname popped up again. Cowboy fans bragged that Troy Aikman and Emmitt Smith would lead America's Team back to the Super Bowl. Sorry, the experts said. The offense is super, but the Cowboys don't have a defense.

The Dallas coaches moved quickly to fix the problem. First they drafted some fast defensive backs. Then they acquired pass rusher Charles Haley. Haley, a three-time player in the **Pro Bowl**, turned out to be a one-man wrecking crew. Thomas Everett, a fine, strong safety, came over from Pittsburgh. The mix of rookies and veterans gave the team its missing defense.

The Cowboys soon passed a big test. The Redskins, defending Super Bowl champs, fell to Aikman and Company, 23–10. Smith carried 27 times for 140 yards. Michael Irvin and Alvin Harper had a field day catching Troy's passes. Haley racked up a sack and forced a fumble.

Picking up speed, the Cowboys rolled over the Giants, 34–28, and Phoenix, 31–20. Then came a Monday night game against Philadelphia. The Eagles harried Troy with a fierce pass rush and won easily, 31–7. Cowboy fans held their breath. Could the young team bounce back?

Seattle came to Texas Stadium to test the Cowboys. The defense responded with seven sacks and shut out the Seahawks, 27–0. After their spirits were restored, the Cowboys swept past Kansas City and the Los Angeles Raiders. Next came a rematch with Philadelphia and Randall Cunningham. The Eagle quarterback was 8–1 in his starts against them.

This time the defense hog-tied the clever Cunningham. On offense, Troy drove the Cowboys 80 and 78 yards to two second-half touchdowns. Smith set up the go-ahead touchdown with a 51-yard run. The 20–10 win helped erase a flock of bad memories.

The team flew to Detroit, eager to avenge last year's play-off loss. A 37–3 win took care of that chore. A week later the Rams kicked two field goals to grab a fourth-quarter lead, 27–23. Dallas had a last-second chance to win, but Troy's end-zone pass fell short. Just like that, the win streak was over.

The Cowboys buckled down. They won three straight before meeting the Redskins again. With only 3:14 to play, the defense put on a gutsy goal-line stand to protect a 17–13 lead. When the offense took the field, the coaches called an ill-fated pass play. Troy dropped back, only to be jarred by a crunching tackle. The ball rolled loose, and a Redskin fell on it in the end zone. The costly turnover handed Washington the game, 20–17.

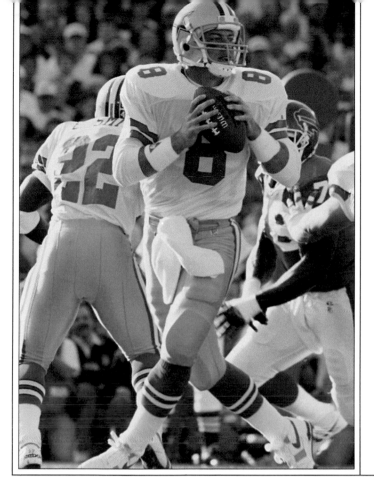

Troy drops back for a quick release during this 1993 play-off game.

The Cowboys shook off the loss and blasted Atlanta, 41–17. With the division title in hand, Johnson looked ahead to the play-offs. Would the Cowboys and their young leader choke? The coach shook his head. "Troy can't be intimidated," he said. "If you think otherwise, you don't know Troy Aikman."

The NFL play-offs brought the Eagles to Texas Stadium on January 10, 1993. What should have been a close game turned into a laugher. Dallas rode Troy's arm, Smith's legs, and a swarming defense to a 34–10 blowout. Afterward the Cowboys felt as though they had won a breakthrough victory. Only the San Francisco 49ers stood between them and the Super Bowl.

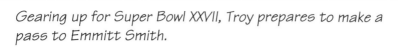
Gearing up for Super Bowl XXVII, Troy prepares to make a pass to Emmitt Smith.

Chapter 10

On Top of the World

The Cowboys went into San Francisco as underdogs. Could Troy find the seams in the 49ers' veteran defense? Babe Laufenberg, a former Dallas quarterback, spoke for the team. "Next to Joe Montana, this is the most accurate passer I have ever seen," he said. "You won't see this guy making many mistakes."

After a rain-soaked first half that ended 10–10, Troy came out firing. First he drove the Cowboys 78 yards to a score. The next series, *Sports Illustrated* said, "was possibly Aikman's finest as a pro." A 9-minute, 14-play, 79-yard drive ended with Troy's scoring pass to Emmitt Smith.

Steve Young, the league's Most Valuable Player (MVP), rallied the 49ers with a touchdown drive of his own. Now the score was 24–17, and the game was on the line. After the kickoff, the Cowboy coaches called a surprise pass play. The 49ers, bunched up to stop the run, were caught off balance. Alvin Harper pulled in Troy's pass and raced to the 49er 10-yard line. Three plays later, Troy tossed to Kelvin Martin for the touchdown. When time ran out with the score 30–20, the Cowboys hugged one another. They were going to the Super Bowl!

January 31, 1993, was Troy Aikman Day in Henryetta. In Pasadena, California, 98,000 people filled the Rose Bowl. Many had paid up to $1,500 per ticket to see the Cowboys take on the Buffalo Bills. This was Super Bowl XXVII, the greatest show in football. The Bills, champions of the American Football Conference, had played in—and lost—the last two Super Bowls.

Dallas kicked off and forced the Bills to punt. The offense ran three plays but failed to make a first down. The first break of the game came on the next play when Buffalo blocked a punt. Moments later, running back Thurman Thomas scored from the 3-yard line. The Bills seemed to be in control, 7–0.

With Troy showing the way, the Cowboys settled down. The offense and defense combined to put 14 quick points on the scoreboard. Troy opened the sequence by throwing to tight end Jay Novacek for a touchdown. One play after the kickoff, quarterback Jim Kelly fumbled when sacked by Charles Haley. Tackle Jimmy Jones picked up the loose ball at the 2-yard line and fell into the end zone. Cowboys 14, Bills 7.

On their next series the Bills drove to the Dallas 4-yard line. After three running plays gained only three yards, Kelly tried a pass. Thomas Everett picked it off. On the next Buffalo series, Kelly went out with a sprained knee. Frank Reich replaced him. With Reich at the controls, Buffalo had come from 32 points behind to beat Houston. The comeback kid promptly led a field goal drive that cut the Dallas lead to 14–10.

Then the roof fell in on the Bills. Starting from his own 28-yard line, Troy produced a score in five plays. Smith set up his touchdown pass with a 38-yard run. Then a fumble by Thomas

Teammates congratulate MVP Troy Aikman for bringing the Cowboys to a Super Bowl victory over the Buffalo Bills.

led to Troy's touchdown pass to Michael Irvin. The Cowboys left the field at halftime with a 28–10 lead.

Pop star Michael Jackson danced for the crowd during a colorful halftime show. When the game resumed, Dallas did most of the dancing. Troy completed four passes in a field-goal drive that took seven minutes off the clock. The Bills fought back, scoring on Reich's 40-yard pass to cut the Dallas lead to 31–17.

That was Buffalo's last gasp. After Troy threw 45 yards for one touchdown, an interception and a fumble led to two more scores. The assault left the Bills looking shell-shocked. The scoreboard read 52–17 when time ran out seven minutes later.

President Bill Clinton displays a Cowboys jersey presented to him by head coach Jimmy Johnson (left) and team owner Jerry Jones (right) during a White House ceremony honoring the Super Bowl champs. MVP Troy Aikman stands second from right.

Chapter 11

The Life of a Superstar

The Super Bowl was over, and the celebration was in full swing. The Cowboys' dressing room rocked with cheers and the pop of champagne corks. Owner Jerry Jones cradled a huge silver trophy. By that time Troy had a prize of his own. His stats—22 completions in 30 attempts for 273 yards and 4 touchdowns— earned him the game's MVP award.

Michael Irvin shook his head when asked if Emmitt Smith should have won the honor. "Emmitt is great, great, great. But Troy Aikman, what that man did...wow!"

A few days later, "that man" flew to Hawaii to play in the Pro Bowl. Next came a victory parade in Dallas marred by fights and a shooting. Fame brings rewards, Troy was learning, but it also has a price.

One of the rewards is a seven-figure income. The money allows Troy to support good causes. To give something back to UCLA, Troy funds a scholarship. He also coaches at the school's summer camp. In the Dallas area the Troy Aikman Foundation supports children's charities. Henryetta, where the high school stands at 1800 Troy Aikman Avenue, has reason to thank him, too. Six weeks after the Super Bowl, the town opened the Troy Aikman Sports Center. Troy kicked off the project with a $20,000 check.

In May 1992, "something popped" in Troy's back during a weight lifting session. A surgeon repaired the injured disk and put Troy on a rehab program. He proved to be a quick healer. By August he was well enough to take part in the Cowboys' preseason practices. With his usual optimism, Troy told his team-mates that he'd be ready for the season opener on September 6. His coaches said they would wait and see.

Troy says he wants to stay with the Cowboys. Now that he's won one Super Bowl, he would like to win two. But even if he retired today, he would still be rated as a superstar. In 1991 *Sports Illustrated* ranked him 9th on its list of the 50 greatest college quarterbacks.

Among the pros, Troy is carving a similar mark. Only the great Johnny Unitas passed for 10,000 yards faster. Unitas did it in 51 games, Troy in 52. Football experts also like Number 8's skill at avoiding interceptions. From mid-December 1992 through the Super Bowl, he threw 137 passes without being picked off. Best of all, his coaches say, Troy Aikman is a winner. Dallas was 26–8 in the last 34 games he played without being hurt.

Fame has been known to lead young athletes astray. Coach Johnson does not think that will happen to Troy. "He is a greater person off the field than he is a player on the field," Johnson says. "And he is a great player."

More Good Reading About Troy Aikman

If you are ever in Henryetta, Oklahoma, stop in at the local McDonald's. You'll see a fine display of Aikman artifacts—photos, football jerseys, posters, and news clippings. If you want to read more about Troy, you'll have to dig for articles in magazines and newspapers. *Sports Illustrated* and *The Sporting News* are good places to start. Many libraries keep back issues of these publications on microfilm or microfiche. Ask your librarian for help.

In *Sports Illustrated*, look for these articles: Bruce Newman, "The Battle to Be Top Gun" (November 14, 1988); Austin Murphy, "A Duel in the Sun" (August 21, 1989); Rick Reilly, "Down and Out" (January 18, 1993); and Jill Lieber, "Most Visible Player" (February 15, 1993).

Sport (July 1992): Randy Galloway—"Riding High"

Inside Sports (January 1993): Greg Garber—"Back in the Saddle"

The Sporting News (February 8, 1993): Paul Attner—"Dawning of a New Doomsday"

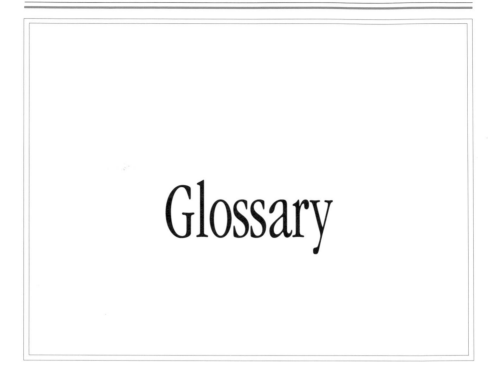

Glossary

agent   A business representative hired by an athlete to negotiate contracts and arrange for endorsements. Agents are paid a percentage of the athlete's income.

All-American   An honorary team made up of the nation's best athletes in a particular sport. All-American teams are picked by sportswriters, coaches, and sports foundations.

club foot   A birth defect in which the feet are misshapen.

football scholarship   Financial aid given to a football player to pay the costs of attending college. In return, the athlete plays football for the college that awards the scholarship.

interception   A forward pass thrown by the offensive team that is caught by a defensive player.

orthopedic shoes   Specially designed shoes that children and adults wear to correct deformities and other foot problems.

play-offs   A series of elimination games in amateur or professional sports. In pro football, they are played by the top teams from the NFL's two conferences. The winners of the NFC and AFC play-offs meet in the Super Bowl.

pocket   The "safe" area that a team's blockers try to create for the quarterback. Pass rushers try to break into the pocket in order to sack the quarterback.

Pro Bowl   A postseason NFL game that matches stars from the NFC against stars from the AFC.

pro draft   A system by which pro teams take turns picking the top college stars from each year's crop of eligible players. The team with the worst record in the previous year drafts first.

redshirt year   A year in which a college player practices with the team but does not play in the team's games. The redshirt year does not count against the player's four years of eligibility.

rookie   An athlete playing for the first time at a more advanced level.

sack   A play in which a defensive player tackles the opposing quarterback before the quarterback can get rid of the ball.

scout   An expert hired by a pro team to evaluate players the team is thinking of drafting.

scrambler   An agile quarterback who confuses defenses by darting quickly from side to side before attempting to pass.

wide receiver   A speedy pass receiver who lines up outside the main offensive formation.

wild card   A team that makes the NFL play-offs on the basis of having the second-best record in its division.

wishbone offense   An option offense in which the quarterback has the choice of running with the ball, pitching to a trailing halfback, or (rarely) passing to an open receiver.

Index